God's Diary

God's Diary

Joaquín Antonio Peñalosa

Translated by
Alvaro de Silva

WILLIAM B. EERDMANS PUBLISHING COMPANY
GRAND RAPIDS, MICHIGAN / CAMBRIDGE, U.K.

© 2002 Wm. B. Eerdmans Publishing Co.
All rights reserved

Wm. B. Eerdmans Publishing Co.
255 Jefferson Ave. s.e., Grand Rapids, Michigan 49503 /
P.O. Box 163, Cambridge CB3 9PU U.K.

Text design by Kevin van der Leek Design Inc.

Printed in the United States of America

07 06 05 04 03 02   7 6 5 4 3 2 1

Library of Congress Cataloging-in-Publication Data

Peñalosa, Joaquín Antonio.
[Señor diaria. English]
God's diary / Joaquín Antonio Peñalosa;
translated by Alvaro de Silva.
p.   cm.
Includes bibliographical references.
ISBN 0-8028-3968-1 (alk. paper)
I. Title.

PQ7298.26.E48 S4613   2002
863'.64 — dc21

2002029471

www.eerdmans.com

CONTENTS

❦ v ❦

Divine Leaves

Alvaro de Silva

Oh! What a thing life is, and how objectless to most of us, unless there were a future. We seem to live and die as the leaves; but there is One who notes the fragrance of every one of them, and, when their hour comes, places them between the pages of His great book.

John Henry Newman,
Letter to Miss Bowles, 13 February 1864

"Only God speaks of God," wrote an early Christian theologian who understood, at least, that talk about God is always dangerous. Despite that fact, there is at any time a disconcerting abundance of books about the divinity, and our age is not an exception. In the last few years, I have seen titles as fantastic as *The Birth of God, A History of God,* and *The Life of God (as Told by Himself)*; there is even a "biography of God," volumes of *Conversations with God*, and one book called *Dancing with God* which I dared not open, afraid it would unveil a much more dangerous activity than merely talking about God or with God. I have seen a book called *Disappointment with God* and another that should make happy the latter's author, called *The Disappearance of God*. There is one on *God's Funeral* and, in perfect logical sequence, another about *The Tomb of God*. Only God is likely to know what may come after that, and just looking at the titles I find myself wondering which, if any, is the Real Thing. This plethora of books about the deity reminds me of a "look-alike" contest for people who looked like Groucho Marx; as the story goes, Groucho Marx himself went and came in *third.* . . .

Humanity never stops trying to come to terms with the divinity, and this little book, a diary of the Eternal Father, is yet another effort at painting God in the colors of the Jewish and Christian Scriptures. *God's Diary* distills the greatest story ever told without missing any of the essential poetry, tragedy, and comedy of the Big Book. It is not, however, Holy Writ condensed, but truly a divine diary — that is, according to the dictionary, "a daily record of matters affecting the writer personally." Diaries are secret, intimate documents, pages we pen for ourselves, for our pleasure or solace, though we may desire others to become our companions in secrecy and surprise. The literary genre befits the Creator. Here is the hidden God but also the God revealed in birds and flowers, in the starry sky and the ocean, in children and in the dignity of free men and women learning how to love or suffering in their loneliness or broken down in their old age or dying at last. Wherever they are, whatever they have become, they are also in the pages of God's diary.

❀   ❀   ❀

Like any other book (the Bible included), this divine diary has its human author, a sort of ghostwriter for God. Joaquín Antonio Peñalosa (1921-1999) was born in San Luis Potosí (Mexico). His scholastic training at the Catholic seminary in no way stifled his poetic spirit. On the contrary, there Peñalosa wrote poems that soon became his first book of poetry, published with the title *Pájaros de la tarde (Birds of the Afternoon)* in 1948. As the story goes, one day the young student of theology paid a visit to his bishop and read a few of his poems. Excited by what he heard, the prelate immediately called the rector of the seminary and said, "These poems by Joaquín Antonio must be published." It was the first of a series of books that have earned Peñalosa much recognition in Mexico.[1]

Peñalosa published several collections of his own poetry, and he was also a scholar, a biographer, and a generous anthologist of his native country's poets. In 1955, he received a doctoral degree at the National University of Mexico, and his bibliography includes some thirty literary studies and anthologies. Ever a popular writer, Peñalosa continued to be a presence in the newspapers and magazines of his country. From 1954 until his death, he wrote a weekly column for *El Sol* (Mexico City) which appeared in fifty-five Mexican newspapers. Despite his love of and gift for words, Peñalosa saw his true vocation, and the best part of his life, in his pastoral work. In San Luis Potosí, he became a builder of churches, an endeavor that culminated in the truest and most beautiful church of all, the *Hogar del Niño*, a school for orphans and abandoned children. Once he wrote to me, "I have three hundred children who eat and get sick and all that, and who never pay a penny; for them I write."

1. Peñalosa's poetry has been collected in *Hermana Poesía: Poesía Completa* (Mexico, D.F.: Verdehalago, 2000).

❈   ❈   ❈

At least for the believer, all things talk about God, espe-
cially after a century that has been described by some writ-
ers and thinkers as the century of the silence of God. And
all truly great books, whether they acknowledge it or not,
talk about God. Often, atheists are the most conspicuous
and persistent talkers about God. It cannot be otherwise.
Here is a simple word that fills the universe with its myste-
rious, unending echo. Even the walls built up to stop it only
seem to spread it evermore. In his *Historical Sketches,* John
Henry Newman said that the word *God* is "a theology in it-
self." "Admit a God," he wrote, "and you introduce
among the subjects of your knowledge, a fact encompass-
ing, closing in upon, absorbing, every other fact conceiv-
able." And you could say about the same if you do not ad-
mit a God. The denial becomes omnipresent. But, is there a
better proof of God's existence than his alleged absence?
Can the madness, the contradictions, the fears, the nihil-
ism, the obsessions of those who wish God not to exist be a
better proof?

Many years ago, for example, one of these critics wrote,
in a fury that seems to have its roots in the hellish landscape
of a tortured soul, "The dead center of existence: when it is

all the same to you whether you read a newspaper article or think of God."[2] I read this aphorism, one that seems to capture the exhaustion of intelligence in some modern thinkers, while translating *God's Diary,* and its arrogant nihilism offered a brutal contrast with the God of Peñalosa. The Mexican poet believes that God not only reads daily newspapers, he keeps a diary. For Peñalosa it is not lacking respect to think of God reading newspapers. His God is eternal, yet absolutely interested in the daily news from planet Earth. Day in and day out, the Eternal Father follows, with an excitement all fathers and mothers have experienced, the great story of his wonderful and beloved creatures, and all the more perhaps when they are not that wonderful or lovable. Peñalosa is also the author of "An Interview with God." When the journalist in that piece asks, "Which is your favorite reading, after the Bible, of course?" the Eternal One, in whom there is no passing of days and nights, answers right away, "The newspaper. What most interests me is the daily paper, because it is the continuation of Creation, what men and women do from what I left already done. I

2. E. M. Cioran, *Tears and Saints,* trans. Ilinca Zarifopol-Johnston (Chicago: The University of Chicago Press, 1995), p. 112. The original work was published in Romania in 1937.

also like poetry, that is, good poetry. The other poetry . . . I forgive it, but I don't look at it."[3]

The Christian God of Peñalosa has an interest not only in the earthly dailies but in earthly diaries, even when they are scribbled on the backs of used envelopes or in broken notebooks. His infinite personal interest never diminishes, never stops, until the end when all human lives become in fact final chapters in the Creator's own Great Book. Indeed, we have been told to rejoice because our names "are written in heaven" (Luke 10:20). In the sunset of each life, if God is trusted with such burden (a trust the saints call "abandonment"), he will see to it that all ends well that began well. In that same "interview" the reporter asks God what he finds amusing in humanity, and God quickly replies, "That in their hurry to become adults they get bored of being children, and then long to be children again. That first they lose their health to make money and immediately lose their money to recover their health. That by thinking anxiously about the future, they neglect their present hour, and thus neither live in the present nor in the future. That they live as if they would never die and die as if they had never lived."[4]

3. In Peñalosa's *El ángel y el prostíbulo* (Mexico, D.F.: Jus, 1975), pp. 100-101.

4. Peñalosa, *El ángel y el prostíbulo,* p. 99.

The divine author is the writer with a Midas touch and can turn tears into joy. The Creator may after all turn despair and depression, tears and complaints, the frustrations of life and all human contradictions, unbearable selfishness, and even self-damnation, into a glorious Book of Life, the great human and divine Comedy, to be admired for all eternity, never to be out of print. "We must trust God; he has already trusted us sufficiently," wrote the French poet Charles Péguy. Peñalosa is a Mexican writer but, like Péguy, he makes God speak so well, with such luminosity and so lovingly, because there is no divine language other than the clear language of innocent love. There is an entry in the *Diary* where we catch God the Father writing at the end of the day about the flowers that he made just "to please myself," a marvelous divine moment reminiscent of Mark Twain's description (in another diary, his *Eve's Diary*) of flowers as "those beautiful creatures that catch the smile of God out of the sky and preserve it." Whether God is writing about "the bird workshop," describing a prodigal son in Guadalajara, or even talking to a recalcitrant atheist, his language is always the language of a lover madly in love. Can anyone look at ants in the usual careless, thoughtless manner after reading in this diary God's recipe to make an ant? Step by step, we hear the voice of God calling into existence that miracle of engineering, "Ant, my daughter, my tiny ant."

At one moment in the diary, immediately after the first murder of an innocent one, God the Father curses all murderers throughout the history of blood, whatever disguise and excuse they may take, and calls fratricides all those who harm their own brothers and sisters. I know as well as Peñalosa the infinite mercy of God and his love for all creatures, even at their worst. Yet God curses them. It is the only brutal divine utterance in a book otherwise full of tenderness and affection even for drug dealers who repent. But the page is in perfect agreement with the God of the Hebrew and Christian Scriptures, and with right reason. God's anger is a way to express the terrible and unbelievable things humans can do to his creatures and his creation.

Yes, the page as it is will disturb the reader in a book in which every letter exudes divine joy in creation. Yet there it is, a page of divine wrath in a diary of tender love, the only page I can see almost torn asunder by the hand of God himself in his disgust at the cruelty of man against man. A painful page for God to write.

Good writers want to make the reader see, and Peñalosa, by making a diarist of God, makes us realize that the same principle applies to God the Author. The Creator-Author rejoices at his own creation and wants those creatures made in his own image, intelligent and free, to see the beauty of what has been made and the overall intention of the Maker. "Do you think so little of a single day of beauty?" asks God in answer to the complaint that flowers wither so quickly. To me it seems the perfect reply, not as a mere *aesthetic* answer to the troubles and afflictions of life but, since God is asking the question, one in the line of *theological aesthetics,* as one of the great modern theologians puts it.[5] In the beauty of a flower or a bird, of the sea or the stars, there is a whole theodicy, a magnificent justification of God. Henry David Thoreau wrote, "Heaven is under our feet as well as over our heads," and a contemporary New Testament scholar writes, "On this basis even a flower can be a witness."[6] The conviction that if God exists, he must be good and just and beautiful and merciful, is a great conquest. To me it seems perhaps the greatest tri-

5. Cf. Hans Urs von Balthasar, *The Glory of the Lord: A Theological Aesthetics,* trans. Erasmo Leiva-Merikakis, vol. 1 (San Francisco: Ignatius Press, 1983), p. 38.

6. Thomas L. Brodie, *The Gospel According to John: A Literary and Theological Commentary* (New York: Oxford University Press, 1993), p. 253.

umph of Christianity. Certainly, that is the God portrayed by Peñalosa. *God's Diary* is a popular yet profound example of this aesthetic theology. Its brevity, encompassing the whole span of history, reinforces that impression. A diary may be composed of all manner of notebooks, scraps of paper, and old used envelopes. It is by this intimate means that Peñalosa reveals the whole Book of Heaven and Earth at once. But the *Diary* also makes visible the divine intention and the scope of history, as in a masterful portrait, and the whole of mankind too, beloved creatures, bathed in the beauty and grace of the eternal Father of all.

To use biblical language, it is impossible for man to see God and live but it is possible not to want to see God. Yet, for the Creator (and hence for the creature too), the important thing is that God sees us. Whether we like it or not, we are part of *God's Diary,* and that is why Peñalosa has several moving pages in it written by creatures and created things. The divine diary, as the diary of a lover, will always remain a dialogue between Creator and creatures, between the Father and his children, even for those who refuse the invitation to such an intimate and generous conversation. God sees us, cares for us, dreams about us, desires with infinite and ardent love to have us with him, like a father, like a mother, like a child, like a lover. Like no other lover.

Whether in this world or the next, in life or in death, his creation is never far away from his joyful and merciful grace.

Reading *God's Diary* reminded me of the last entry in another diary, a truly human one, *The Diary of a Country Priest,* by Georges Bernanos: "How easy it is to hate oneself! True grace is to forget. Yet if pride could die in us, the supreme grace would be to love oneself in all simplicity — as one would love any one of those who themselves have suffered and loved in Christ." Just as the priest in that great novel is about to die, deprived of the "final consolations" of his Church, he murmurs to a friend in perfect trust and abandonment, "Does it matter? Grace is everywhere. . . ."

A Little Prologue in Sol Minor

Could the author please tell us why he gave this little book, which is a mere sketchbook, seed of an encyclopedia, rambling notes for a symphony in sol major, the title of God's Diary, *that is,* The Diary of the Eternal Father?

I called it *Diary* because it is a narrative of what has happened with the passing of days even before there were any watches. This is the record of a love story. The real love story. For instance: he lit your desperate heart with hope on Monday, then made round an orange on Tuesday to quench your thirst, on Friday he accepted his son's death that you might live, and on Sunday he made the sun come out after three rainy days not to spoil your vacation in the country.

Now, about fathers and mothers, well, there are parents who generate or procreate another of their kind whom they call son or daughter. There are also those who are "fathers of the nation" because through their bravery and sacrifice they saved their own people. There is the holy father in Rome. And fathers of an immortal book, of a scientific discovery, of a work of art, all children of genius and beautiful intelligence.

All these are fathers with a small f. The protagonist of this diary is the Father. I underlined with red ink all the times Christ said Father in the Gospel. It was the word he repeated most.

God the Father is the most mysterious and the most simple of all realities. This is what the French novelist Balzac experienced: "I understood God a little bit more the moment I had a child myself."

Would the author tell us how he wrote these pages?

The recipe is brief, my dear sir. Listen. Take a cooking pan and put in it a teaspoon of Bible, then add a few drops of filial love, and slowly dust it all with a bit of lyrical intuition. Put all these ingredients in the blender, say an Our Father, and there you have it, a cocktail called God's Diary.

The author would love this cocktail to taste a bit like manna dropped at sunrise to help the pilgrim in the daily journey through the desert in search of the promised land; but he is happy enough if it tastes like mint.

It is much easier to come close to God the Father than to

define him. It is much easier to surround him with an embrace than to try to comprehend him with a syllogism. God the Father is the most mysterious being and the most loving of all.

(Thank you, my child. You're welcome, Father.)

San Luis Potosí, August 15, 1989

The First Record

In our heavenly residence and enjoying full eternity, gathered in permanent session my Son, the Holy Spirit, and this your servant, we resolve, unanimously — we are always unanimous — that we are ready to create the world.

It is going to be a real novelty: there will be time, there will be space, there will be history books with colorful illustrations. In the second item of the day's agenda, we decided that there would even be men and women.

Since we didn't have any other business at hand, we closed the session and proceeded to draw up the agreement.

Thus I myself attest, the Eternal Father.

(The angel custodian of archives, wings fluttering, did nothing but repeat: "Men and women, men and women, what can these be?")

My Name

What a long litany, what a cascade of names they have given me! Socrates — who spent his life in the streets of Athens teaching virtue and wisdom, called me "Supreme Intelligence That Sets All Things in Order"; Aristotle — I also call him "The Intelligence," as his teacher Plato named him — called me "Pure Act," "Immobile Mover," "Absolute Perfection." All these names, after being made sublime, were taken to the highest degree of exaltation by my friend Thomas Aquinas, who was a *summa* in everything, beginning with his rotund body.

But don't you think these names are a bit too much, I mean, too metaphysical? The "Being that subsists by itself," the "Uncaused Cause"? And besides, metaphysics doesn't love anyone, and ignores a good burning, the joy of fire with its golden tuft.

I do like the way the Aztecs described me, though, those Aztec poets whose verses are like pretty birds in their marvelous plumes colored with tones of turquoise and jade, like water flowers, or like bracelets of precious stones.

They called me the "Giver of life," the "Lord by whom all things live," the "Inventor of humans beings" — you can already feel blood singing in the branching off of veins; the "God of the Great Truth," the "Lord of Close By and Near at Hand" — never far away, never; and that precious appellative that moves me so deeply: God is "Night-and-Wind." Night and wind are invisible, impalpable, but there they are acting in their living presence. But I like best the name that Jesus always used to address this his servant: "Father." And the "Our" in "Our Father" is not the result of adding up many "my"'s. "Our" comes before "my" and "mine," precedes personal invocations and makes them possible.

So, what's my full name? "Our Father to serve you all."

This Beard of Mine

"What I cannot do," the sculptor told me, "is carve your beard. For the eyes I found inspiration in lightning. And there they are, like flashes of lightning that have stopped on their descent, frozen, burning. But your beard. Your beard is what defines you. A beardless Eternal Father is not the Eternal Father. What do you think I should do?"

"Get rid of that thin, soft beard with its naive and permanent swinging effect. Forget that rivulet that looks like a girl going down the stairs giggling. I want the ocean. I want a beard like a swelling sea, a rough tempest, a volcano of a beard fully bursting into sparks, a rainstorm of beards that may sound without stopping seventy times seven thunderclaps; perhaps a cloud, immensely cloudy and immensely bearded, or a golden wheat field nine acres large, or Niagara Falls, with waters boiling in thunder. A beard such that when my hand caresses it, a forest of magnolias will spring up, if the beard is white; if red, let the sun rise right there setting the morning aflame; and if black, let the night appear in all its thickness."

"Eternal Father, won't children be afraid of your beard?"

"My beard is cradle and caress, like a dovecote of stars."

(And the thick, long, river-like, flowing beard broke out in two golden wings.)

The Photo Album

"I'd like to catch a glimpse of what you look like, Eternal Father, although I know that the ocean does not fit in a mother-of-pearl shell. Is there a talking picture? At least, a sort of snapshot? Where can we find goodness more or less resembling your infinite goodness? All things on earth have a stain. The sun has its spots; the moon, its quarter; and there are pores in the marble of the Greek statues. Which telescope, which brush, which cable-television network, which big chunk of the universe, which saint's heart can take us closer to your figure?"

Eternal Father remained quiet. Then he granted the word to Jesus: "He who sees me sees the Father" (John 14:9).

(Jesus is his photograph, natural size and full color.
The exact replica. The perfect mold. Live television.)

Garden Angelica

"Let there be angels." I am writing in my diary what I have created today. And so the angels began to be. Thousands of thousands, legions, like a whirlwind of stars, living galaxies. My own home suddenly inhabited by spiritual creatures, most intelligent and free, my precious and powerful children. They adore me, my messengers, and they will do many things for me.

"You, Cherub, station yourself at the gates of Paradise with a flaming sword to shut out those who would enter" (Genesis 3:24).

"Move quickly, Sentinel Angel, I need you on Mount Moriah where Abraham is about to sacrifice his son. Shout at him, stop his knife" (Genesis 22:10-11).

"You, Swift Athletic Angel, ambush Jacob, fight with him all night, dislocate his hip joint and, at sunrise, bless your adversary because he has fought undauntedly with an angel" (Genesis 32:24-31).

"Raphael, please, guide the son of Tobias my servant. He is on his way to claim his father's money in foreign lands. Take a stick with you and also a knapsack." (Sorry, Father, what's that?) "A bundle, a traveling bag for food and things" (Tobit 5:4-5).

"You, Federal Express Angel, Air Mail Angel, Special Delivery Angel, fly to Bethlehem to tell the shepherds the good news that their Savior has just been born for them" (Luke 2:10-11).

"Angel, Most Full of Compassion, look at Jesus in his anguish in the Garden of Olives: sweat like drops of blood streams down his body to the ground. Comfort him" (Luke 22:43-44).

"And you, my little Paschal Angel. Yes, you, with face like lightning and that floating tunic made of snowflakes, move aside the stone by the sepulcher, sit on top of it, and announce that the Dead One on the Cross has risen" (Matthew 28:2-3).

Do you know how the heavenly angels who look at my face will know the sunrise and sunset on earth? Because when children get up and when they go to sleep, their chubby little hands together, they will pray as if singing this line: "Guardian angel of mine, my sweet company, do not abandon me, neither during the day nor in the night."

(And thus they will fall asleep, sucking their thumbs
while dreaming of angels more wonderful than those by
Fra Angelico, Raphael, Leonardo, el Greco, Rembrandt,
Chagall; ah, and that swarm of chubby-cheeked cheru-
bim by Murillo.)

Let There Be Light

Let there be light, my firstborn creature of the earth, so
that when the caretaker arrives, the house may be well lit,
so that he will not stumble.

How beautiful you are, my dear girl, how beautiful you
are, your ears bedecked with earrings, your neck with
necklaces.

You will be a strange being, almost absent as it were.
No one will be able to touch you, nor will you allow them
to possess you. Flee, virginal and elusive, from the hand
that may try to take hold of you. Oxygen they can store,
but never light.

I want you chaste as white lilies among thorns, discreet to the point of seeming almost nonexistent, free from any ties, living only for those who may give themselves to you with eyes full of infinite love.

How beautiful you are, my child. They are going to fall in love with you at just one of your glances, with just one turn of your neck.

To be born will be to bring another to the light. To wake up, to return to the light after the unconsciousness of sleep. To die, to come in possession of light.

(Father, can it be true? A scientist has written that the majority of plants nourish themselves with only thirty percent water and earth, and seventy percent light. Are plants and forests condensed light? Green light which, like traffic lights, signals and makes possible for us to go on living?)

I, the Sea

The Eternal Father said, "Let the waters under the heavens be gathered together unto one place, and let the dry land appear. And it was so. And I called the dry land earth; and the gathering together of the waters, I called sea" (Genesis 1:9-10).

Now, I, the Sea, talk to you, Father. The Sea just born gives you thanks for having made me after your own likeness: deep, unfathomable, unique, ever new, mighty, unutterable, full of life, everywhere present, immense, without limits.

Not even I know whether that blue of the horizon is still me, the Sea, or is already the sky that begins. A ship could likewise make a mistake and, instead of following me, continue upward and upward risking never to return, lost forever, because the sky is also immense and without bounds.

Perhaps you did not put your signature on me because I am a snowy rose of shifting foam. But, upon seeing me, they will say, "Truly, one can feel that the author is you, Father."

Praised Be the Fire

Praised be you, my child, the Fire. I make you good and terrible. And necessary. I would like you to be useful only to make bread — there is no bread without fire. And thus, young people would gather to sing together around a bonfire of red-hot plumes. How can you call anything life if we do not live it together? How can it be life if we do not shake hands? If we do not sing the same song, though the voices may be different?

Expel the darkness, my child, the Fire, so that no one may stumble and fall. Warm deep, to the marrow, to the very bones and souls of so many cold and lonely men and women, deprived of love. I make you huge that you may be a star, or small that you may be a match. A match is a portable star, a pocket star.

Days will come when men who don't know how to hold hands, nor how to sing together around a bonfire, will want to use you for burning, for war, for destruction. Oh, my good and terrible child.

Today, the Fourth Day

Today I made two big luminaries, the lord Sun to rule the day and the lady Moon — so beautiful! — to rule the night, and in addition a stream of stars, so that the heavens looked like a blue garden of golden daisies. I was happy and content with what I had made (Genesis 1:14-19).

But the sky will not always remain so beautiful. One day the Space Era will begin with the launching of the first Soviet sputnik, and my children will fill what had been a clean vault with garbage. As Pablo Neruda will say,

Roads walked upon before by saints,
are now inhabited by specialists.

There will be twenty thousand objects in orbit and millions of particles dangerously floating in the blue sky, voyagers like metallic fish swimming in a tomb-like silence, archers of satellites, divers returned to the belly of space capsules; weightless, floating, stellar, astronauts; creatures of the fourth day which does not end; praised be you all for leaving pride behind in that microscopic village called Earth to regain, in space, your correct measure of smallness. With my son Dante, praise the Love that moves the Sun and the stars.

The Bird Workshop

Eternal Father took in his hands a piece of paper, made an origami bird, threw it up into the air for a flight, and the paper bird quickly nailed its beak to the ground.

Eternal Father took a bit of cotton, fashioned a little, soft, cottony bird, launched it for a flight, and the little bird remained immobile upon a branch.

Eternal Father took some plaster in his hands, modeled a curly crested bird, put inside the New York Symphony — or perhaps a little music box? — and dressed it up with red feathers in its breast until it looked like a cardinal entering Saint Peter's in Rome. Painted voice, winged song. He kissed its rosy beak. Ah, wings, what are you for? The flying orchestra fled the Eternal Father's hands, "a joyful speed dividing the air with a keel of songs."

Look at the birds that put the sky between quotation marks, singing flowers, flowers that fly. They don't know how to plant nor how to harvest, they lack tractors and warehouses. My Father feeds them with an à la carte menu: small grains of wheat, little worms made of light, drops like eyes of water; and for dessert, honey from the hive.

A Recipe to Make an Ant

I am going to take some time to make small creatures, the kind of creatures that only a magnifying glass and a few poets can really see. And thus I will also please a saint who will write in the Middle Ages, "Eternal Father is great in great things, and greatest in small things." Pretty sentence.

My God, where should I begin? "My God," that's me, of course. Shall I begin with the grains of white sand in the beach or with a garden snail? Aha, I know.

Here I put a rounded little head, no bigger than a pin-head; I place two microscopic fine eyes, then add the thorax and abdomen; now a pair of high fidelity antennae and strong mandibles that it may eat well; here I fix some strong legs because I want it to be a traveler, a forerunner of those who will march in walking demonstrations and of Formula One race cars too. Ah, I must design a perfect reproductive apparatus: I don't want this pretty miniature to live alone, but in colonies of a hundred thousand, of five hundred thousand individuals. And now I have to bathe it in color; I have several to choose from: red, white, and black. Would black be too elegant? Let me take my miniature's measurements. That's it, a quarter of an inch of life, a quarter of an inch of tenderness. And its name? I baptize you as "the Ant."

Ant, my little daughter, I want you to be hardworking, provident, constructive. You will be able to excavate the earth and protect your kind in a bunker of perfect humidity and ventilation, interior castles with immense galleries and labyrinths of intricate networks. There you will create warehouses for food, incubators for the newly born, chambers for cultivation, warm bedrooms, living rooms. The only thing that bothers me a little bit is the wise scientist who will come giving you such a long and ugly name: "A Hymenopterus insect of the family Formicidae."

(Eternal Father placed the miniature in the infinite palm of his hand: "Ant, my daughter, my tiny ant.")

A Professorship in April

Today I am just going to please myself making flowers. Superb, minuscule, of the garden variety, aquatic, climbers, princesses, gothic, surrealists, ceremoniously dressed, modest, flirting, disguised as birds, mad with joy, loop collections, eau de cologne, little boxes of pollen, lace made of snow, cold fires, smiles of the earth, flasks of perfume, bride's muslin, Ph.D.'s in cosmetology, constellations of diamonds, fashionably dressed, twins of butterflies, airfields for bees, confetti in the long hair of trees, all the lights and colors of sapphire; "to be a flower is to be a bit of color with the breeze."

They don't know how to embroider, don't knit with two needles, don't have a Singer machine; but I have seen flowers so luxuriously dressed up that not even Christian Dior could equal them in his best collection.

"Eternal Father, Father floriculturist, why so much squandering in a simple flower that barely lasts one day?"

"Do you think so little of a single day of beauty? A flower quickly withers, it is true, but its aroma remains. It withers quickly, but immediately another one opens. Late in the day, 'there will be no roses, but our sight will preserve forever their burning fires.'"

Here He Is

Today Adam asked how I made him. "I am also a potter," I told him. "First I modeled you in clay, clay from the ground, then I breathed into your nostrils the breath of life" (Genesis 2:7).

"When I opened my eyes," Adam replied, "I saw you at my side and, right away, I knew that it was you who had made me: you were smiling. And then the first word I said was 'Father'."

Adam asked me, "Why, having so many shining things

on earth, did you make me? Was it not enough for your recreation to have the waves that the sea plays with, the collection of emeralds that is the forest, the handfuls of stars that frost the tips of your fingers?"

"You know what? I felt lonely, in need of communion."

Then he knew that even God, being God, wants a friend.

Because It Is Night

"What is this, Father? Is the world that you made coming to an end or have you blinded me? What is this, Father?"

"It is the night, Adam. Your first night."

"How terrible is this demotion. I can't even see my own hands. 'The cluster of trees drinking in the stream' has disappeared, and so have the roses that look like blown glass, and the clouds, and my little star-colored dog. All that remains of Paradise is a cold heap of shadows. Now I know that the day's treasures were vain."

"Don't curse the night, Adam. Night is rest. Silence. Sleep. Only during the night can you hear the birth of the fountainhead in the forest."

"But tell me if this will end. When does the night finish? You have left me absent from the world, outside my home, lost in an infinite tunnel. Blind and terrified. What have you done with the sun, Father?"

"Do not worry, Adam, it will return."

Then Adam could say no more. The first sleep fell upon him under the night sky.

꧁꧂

Profession: Gardener

Genesis 2:8-15

Today I planted a garden. I made grow out of the ground all manner of trees, some astonishingly beautiful to the sight and others delicious to taste. Not everything on earth has to be utilitarian and functional. To behold the flower of the peach tree shall be as necessary as eating the peach.

Immediately I called Adam.

"You are going to live in this garden so that you may dress it and guard it. Eternal Father does not like idleness. And so, the first blessing I give you is work. You will be happy acting as gardener and forester."

❦❦❦❦❦❦❦❦❦

A Fashion Show of Furs and Feathers

Genesis 2:19-20

"Adam, my son, let me introduce to you the domestic animals, the birds of the heavens and the wild beasts that I have just given shape to, so that you may give them names. To name is to singularize. Thus it will be easier to study zoology, and children going to the circus will not confuse a lion with a leopard. I hope your imagination may work like the poet's imagination. A poet is one who gives names to things."

"You who play being a flower, your name is Purple Heron."

"And you, millimetric sort of tape to measure the fields, you shall be Snail."

"Peacock, large brilliancy, you walk by the democratic henhouse as a royal procession."

"Receive the name of Cricket, because you splinter the night with your monochord and simple violin."

"You, sleepwalker and hollow-eyed? Owl, of course."

"Watch out for that Scorpion that comes out from some corner, a slithery shape in between a parenthesis and a question mark."

"Name yourself as you please, Sea-gull, piece torn from the water's foam or moving snow in the wind."

"I baptize you Tiger; you carry ingots of gold on your skin or the iron bars of a cage."

"Eternal Father, do you like the name of Zebra for that little ass made of such pure fantasy that I don't know whether it is white with black stripes or black with white stripes?"

"You will have names of heavy machinery: Mastodon, Dinosaur, Mammoth, Buffalo, Hippopotamus."

"And you? *Colibri*, hummingbird, the garden's helicopter. Next? Butterfly, because you're sentimental, carrying a postcard from flower to flower. You, such a chatterer? Parrot. For that skyscraper with wall-to-wall carpet, I like Giraffe. And that one looking at me with caressing eyes, let it be Dog."

It was a parade of furs and feathers the likes of which the jet set will never see at Paris or New York fashion shows. Only She, precisely the one for Adam, was missing in the long parade, the Woman.

"Give her to me, Eternal Father."

"Go to sleep, my child. It's easy to dream . . . ."

She

Genesis 2:18-23

"Adam, it is not good for you to be alone. I am going to make you a companion, one like you."

I covered Adam with drowsiness and he fell asleep. What a surprise he will have when he awakens, I thought.

When he woke up, Adam fell as into another dream just by looking at the woman. So radiant and so much like him, this woman.

"Adam, don't tell me I am not a feminist. Woman was my idea to begin with."

"But why at the very end, Father?"

"Like a fitting end for a festivity, like a happy ending for a movie, like one who puts his signature upon his finished work. What do you think of your wife?"

"This one is indeed bone of my bones and flesh of my flesh."

(Adam got closer to Eve and took her by the hand with a smile. Right then and there were born love, the kiss, the child, courtship and romance, and sixty percent of the poetry that has been written in the world. A pair of doves flew toward the nest in the blue light.)

Day of Rest

Tomorrow is the seventh day, and I have decided that I will not write even one word in the Diary of the Eternal Father. Blank page. Since I have finished that which I began to make, I will take the day off.

The First Child Is Born

Father,

My wife and I would like to let you know — though you may already know it — that this morning our first child was born, exactly as you foretold Eve after the fall: "You will give birth in pain." It was a long scream.

The child was born crying — but why? The morning was a feast of roses and doves. He weighs nine pounds, he has the same mysterious eyes as his mother, his father's forehead. We have given him the name of Cain.

We want to surrender our son to you — that is, we want to surrender your son. You want us to be partners with you in your creative fecundity; you allow us to share in your paternity.

Looking at this rosy flesh, those fine little eyes drooping with sweetness. We feel happy, but we are afraid. We have given him as our inheritance blood and sin. May he be a good child.

ADAM AND EVE

Nomads and Dwellers

Genesis 4:2

This morning I saw, from a distance, the boys working. How they have grown up!

Cain chose the fields, he is a farmer. There he is from sunrise to sunset, drowned in the surging waves of the wheat fields, rooted in the land and its fruits, running the risk of becoming a slave to a land that is by its very nature possessive. The land bends the worker.

Abel is a shepherd. To and fro he comes and goes with the restless flock, from the peaks to the valleys, from the pastures to the brooks, from the shepherd's lodge to the distant mountain peaks where sheep of full udders graze, and a buck shows its head up, proud and defiant, against the innocence of the clouds.

Cain is static; Abel, dynamic. Cain is the sojourn, Abel the journey. Cain is the arriving point, Abel the point of departure. Cain is still; Abel is a nomad. Cain looks to the ground right below; Abel to the blue without boundaries.

From now on, thus will men be divided. Some will be like Cain the dweller in the land and others like Abel the inventor of pathways.

(I see, far in the distance, a new Abel, restless walker and shepherd, innocent victim, ah, my Son.)

The First Pietà

Genesis 4:3-12

You are sleeping on my lap, Abel, my son. But your child-like face is today a cold grimace. A little while ago you said to me, "I'm going to the fields with my brother." What a handsome young man you were, offering the Father your best sheep, silk-like and so full of wool. Your brother envied you. What are we going to do, Adam, with this fallen fruit, all cracked and stinking? What does one do with a corpse?

Today I have learned in one blow what tears are all about — the sea has less salt — , what is to cry and yell and for no use at all, how sweet and terrible it is to be a mother, what is death, this bulldozer which leaves behind paralyzed and blind and crushed the one who goes and those who remain.

Father, first I lost one paradise; today I have lost two. Tell me for whom should I cry more, for the son who has been murdered or for the son who is the murderer? I hear your enraged voice:

"What have you done, Cain? Your brother's blood is crying to me from the earth. You shall be cursed by the earth that opened its mouth to receive your brother's blood from your hand. Even when you till the ground, it will not yield unto you its strength. A fugitive and a vagabond shall you be on the earth."

"Sleep on my lap, Abel, my son. Sleep on, my little one, my little lamb, my lost paradise . . . ."

Do Not Grow Old

I'm going to put down in my *Diary* what Eve told me in her prayer today.

"You know well by now, Father, that my husband is quickly growing old. His legs are so swollen and hurt that he barely walks; he forgets about things, sleeps poorly, nothing interests him, and everything is bad for him. The only thing he can digest is the applesauce I prepare for him every day. You described to me once the handsome Adam that a great artist named Michelangelo will one day paint in the Sistine Chapel, but I'm sure no one who gazes at that image would recognize Adam as he looks today. Nothing but bones remain, and wrinkles too, and melancholy eyes like half-closed shutters. Father, what a terrible thing it is to grow old!"

Then I spoke to her heart.

"Eve, my daughter, neither are you that young woman in Paradise performing her dramatic role like a shining star. To grow old is to go up, to go up and up toward the life that never ends. To grow old is to vanquish time. Learn to grow old without becoming old. It is always time to dream, to work, to love. Blessed are the young in spirit, because they will never grow old."

(Eve pondered in her heart the words of the Father. With applesauce in hand, she went to her aging husband and Adam smiled at her. "How beautiful the green that still remains in a dry leaf.")

A Question Without an Answer

Some time ago, after Cain had killed Abel, I reprimanded him with a question: "What have you done with your brother?"

And Cain, making bold: "I don't know. Am I my brother's keeper?" (Genesis 4:9).

Every day I have to hear that same elusive phrase of the murderer: "I don't know." No one wants to take responsibility for his brother's death, but all are accomplices.

Fratricides are all of you. Abortionists who kill with premeditation, treacherously and at advantage; drug dealers and their underground empire where the sun doesn't set; fetid pornographers carrying tons of magazines and videocassettes; merchants of human flesh, more profitable when more innocent, I curse you all. Imperial wolves who subdue and abuse weak nations with unpayable loans. Manufacturers of bullets, machine guns, and skeletons. Those who raise the price of corn, wheat, and sugar to hungry people almost dead from starvation. Those collectors of dollars and diamonds whose pockets can never be filled. Those who destroy hope, conscience, and the dawn: daily Cains, murderers. Listen to me.

I gave you a brother that you might love him for me and yet you turn your back on him time and time again. Your brother's blood is crying to me from the ground.

⁂

Patched-Up Men

No, Father, we are not coming from the war, we are coming from life, which also leaves us battered and unrecognizable.

"My eyes, made of glass; I can't see with them, but at least they make me less monstrous."

"My teeth, artificial teeth; with them I can still savor the taste of bread, like ground gold, and of figs 'like the crepuscule, most sweet and somber.'"

"My iron leg, whose hooks, hinges, and screws allow me to walk, one little step upon another, through the poplars in the park."

"The little device hidden behind my ear with which I

can hear the wind, the shrill of the cricket, the ringdove, the song by Edith Piaf."

"The soft and brownish wig that covers my most illustrious and most reverend baldness, protecting me from frosts, summer dog days, and the stubborn skidding of flies."

"The pacemaker that continues to mark the beating of my worn heart."

We are made of plastic, metal, glass, wires, definitely artificial and fictitious, more children of technology than of our holy mother. Father, do you recognize us?

And the Eternal Father responded, "I made you in my image and likeness. Intelligent and free."

⁂

An Interview via Satellite

Why do you call yourself Father?

Not only do I call myself Father, I am Father. For two reasons: because I generate my Eternal Son of the same divine nature, light from light; and because I adopt all human beings as my own children. I have a natural son and millions of adopted children.

Why is the Eucharist so careful about asking us to say, "We have the daring to say, *Our Father*"?

Well, because it really is daring to call God "Father," yet this is the marvelous reality that Jesus taught you, isn't it? Do you know Aramaic?

Just a bit of English, Father.

I'm asking you because when Jesus taught the Lord's Prayer, he began the supplication with the Aramaic word *Abba*. The English word *Father* does not express the shade of meaning Jesus engraved in that word. *Abba* is much closer to your *Dad*.

Are you a sweet father or an irascible one? Paternal or avenging?

Those are caricatures, not the real photograph. My justice has never stopped being merciful.

Describe your love to me.

Read the Bible. I caress and comfort my child upon my knees (Isaiah 66:12-13). I press my baby against my face (Hosea 11:4). I wipe away all tears from their eyes (Revelation 21:4). Can a woman forget her suckling child, the fruit of her womb? Well, even if she may forget — a monstrous thought — yet will I not forget you (Isaiah 49:14-15). The very hairs of your head are all numbered, and not even one of them will fall without my permission (Matthew 10:30).

(We conclude today's interesting interview with our usual sign-off: "Love doesn't say, This is mine. It says, This is yours.")

A Poetry Contest

To all the poets of the Heavenly Court,

I cordially invite you to participate in the First Eternal Poetry Contest (that is, poetry that is never out of fashion). The themes and extension of the poems are absolutely free.

Authors will submit their work to Saint Teresa of Avila who lives now in the seventh and very last mansion. The prize, one and indivisible, will consist in having greater glory for all.

The jury, whose judgment is beyond appeal, will be comprised of Saint John of the Cross, also known as "Flame of Living Love," Sister Juana Inés de la Cruz, née "Tenth Muse," and Dante Alighieri, if he has already returned from his visit to hell and purgatory.

Signed,
Eternal Father

A Choir of Angels

The angels had been trilling for an eternity. They were singing psalms, antiphons, hosannas, and glorias, in the same two voices, in four different voices, a cappella, in Gregorian chant, in Palestrina-like polyphony, accompanied by harps and lutes and soft flutes, mixing *fortissimo*

with *molto vivace* and *pizzicato*. They even wanted to per-
form a rock opera called "From Genesis to Apocalypse,"
just like that, while several holy hermits, unaccustomed to
such high decibel levels, could by no means concentrate on
their meditation.

Eternal Father lifted his voice over the choir of angels:

"Do you not know that silence is also a way to praise
God?"

Musical scores, music stands, instruments, throats, all
shut down. Not even the tiny bird of glory was singing.
The only sound left was the supplication of silence in sol
sharp major.

Miss Mary

"I just came back, Eternal Father. I bring you good news
on the matter you entrusted to me. Oh! she is so beautiful.
I'm sure you made her according to your taste, in agree-
ment of course with the Son and the Holy Spirit. I was go-

ing to tell you she looks like an angel, but, not at all, she surpasses all of us together. I, Gabriel, am very small before her.

"'Good morning, Miss Mary,' I said to her. 'Rejoice, full of grace, God is with you.' I noticed her baffled at my greeting, after such a cascade of praises and compliments. I don't mean that I scared her, being from another world as I am, no, but that she felt very small like a leaf of mint, disturbed by her own humility. What shall I do, holy Father, to take this impression away from her?

"'Be not afraid, precious girl. Eternal Father sends me to tell you that he loves you very much and that you are going to be the mother of his son, the savior of the world, and that you should give him the name of Jesus. How do you like it?' She didn't say either yes or no. She was thinking, thinking. How long did that silence last? To me it felt like an eternity, like the eternity I was coming from. Thanks to God, we angels are not impatient. Miss Mary had a perfect right to reflect and clear all doubts."

"'How can I be a mama if I have had no relationship with any man?'"

"'Understand, nothing is impossible for God. There is no need at all for any man; God alone will act. The Holy Spirit will make you fruitful. What do you think?'

"Oh, Eternal Father, I felt so tiny while waiting for her answer. If the young lady says no, what will my Father think — that I couldn't manage the business he entrusted to me? And the Son is going to be left in the waiting room, his turn never arriving. And humanity will be left without the Savior. Oh, dear God of my life, what straits one has to go through while on earth."

Then she spoke: "'I am the servant of the Lord, be it done unto me according to what you have told me.'"

"I was so happy with her acceptance that I immediately took off to come back and give you the news, Father. My joy was such that I don't remember whether I said good-bye to Mary. . . ."

("Let's check in the Gospel of Luke: 'And the angel departed from her,' Luke 1:38. Good heavens, dear God! Shame on me for not having said good-bye to the queen of the angels.")

The Two Fathers

Matthew 1:18-25

I want to register in my diary the confidence that Joseph showed in me today, the young craftsman born in Bethlehem and descendant of King David, who is so close to me, like my shadow:

"Father, I went to bed last night saddened to death; but an angel of yours came in a dream — what jets of light surrounded him — and I woke up as if my skin were bursting with spring, as if the marrow of my bones was flowering with jasmine.

"I had told her with my lips and with my soul, 'I love you, Mary.' And she, like a pure, caressing breeze, 'I love you, Joseph.' Then one day I saw her bulky belly and the world fell down on me. I decided to leave her. To leave her. Only you, Eternal Father, are a just judge. I would go, purposely lost and lonesome, to ruminate and grow old like a camel in the desert, or else to take refuge in the occupational therapy of my carpentry.

"'Don't suffer,' your angel told me last night, 'take

unto you Mary, your wife.' (I was relishing every word: my wife, mine, mine.) 'The creature in her womb comes by the Spirit. She is to have a son and you' (I, Lord?), 'you are to name him Jesus because he will save his people from their sins.'

"You entrust to me your son made man that I may give him civil status, family, a genealogical tree, country, home, bread, a coat, language, education, work, the craftsman's social class, protection, love. Today my heart grew large and deep and clear like Lake Tiberias in Galilee. I am a father. Because a few minutes are enough for a man to be a progenitor but a whole life is not enough to be a father. Only you and I will be called 'father' by Jesus, and he will throw his arms around my neck, hugging me like the ivy that covers the tree trunk with green kisses.

"The red-fingered angel flapped its wings and went out. When I woke up, I went to see Mary, took her by the hand, and the two of us spoke, without words, of an infinite joy. We looked into each other with a smile. Let's go, Mary. (Trees were asking each other, from one bird to another, 'Who are these lovers?')"

What beautiful wood is he taking to the shop. Saint Mary and Saint Joseph they will now be called.

A Tent to Dwell In

Earlier today I wrote in my diary, *To love is to give. You know how to love when you know how to give. The greater the love, the greater the gift.* Since my love for you, men and women, is infinite, my gift for you must be infinite. I give you my only Son (John 3:16).

If among you a father were to give away his son, and that son were his only child besides, you would reprehend such a parent as ungrateful and unnatural. But I give you my Son; he is yours without ceasing to be mine. Therefore, call him brother, treat him like a brother. Call on him in a familiar way.

Today, therefore, at zero hour — first day, first year of the Christian era — my Son took flesh and made his tent to dwell among you.

A Voice in the River

Matthew 3:13-17

This morning, under a scorching sun, I saw Jesus walking toward the east shore of the Jordan. He has already grown into a real man. Strong, youthful. He must be thirty years old.

Rivers are roads that walk. The Jordan springs forth in the slopes of Mount Hermon and, after blue turns and fanciful circles through deserts and valleys, hastens into the Dead Sea. (Our lives are rivers marching into the sea that is Love.)

John has baptized many, but I saw how he resisted baptizing the white, white, white Lamb. Jesus insisted. He untied his sandals, took off his cloak and his tunic, and went down to the river to be immersed and baptized.

Coming out of the water, the Spirit descended like a dove upon Jesus. I, the Eternal Father, said with a robust voice, full of emotion, "This is my Son, whom I love, my beloved one." Yes, it was a word of pleasure and gratification; but also an accolade for my Son at the beginning of his mission.

(The people were thinking, saying, "Descending into
the waters of the Jordan you enter into our lives. Bap-
tism is your second birth, your second descent. For us
it is a way of departure, a liberation from evil; for you it
is a way of entering into the fall, into the tunnel of
darkness, this world of ours. What kind of water did
you take from the river? Blue water like a drink made of
turquoise, or muddy water from a quagmire? You took
the sins we had left there, well within the river of life.")

A Message for the Sun

Sun, my child, open your eyes, it's already dawning. Get
up, sleepy one. Come on, put on your red space suit and
spread out your golden rays like a fan. Please, light up all
men and women without exception, be they good or bad,
capitalists or socialists, chaste or double adulterers, just or
unjust. Make no distinction between friends and foes. Bet
only for love.

(On the TV News at 7 P.M., Boston: "The elderly at the nursing home were delighted sunbathing in the garden." Cienfuegos, Cuba: "The sun continues to favor the golf-green-colored plantations." Buenos Aires: "The sunny Argentinian flags sprang forth to brighten the South Pole.")

Lord of the Rain

"Your Father who is in heaven sends his rain on the just and on the unjust" (Matthew 5:45).

Do you know, Father, what impresses me most in this sentence of Jesus in the Gospel? The possessive adjective "his." You are the lord of the rain.

You keep it in safes in the clouds. Cottony clouds, indigo prairies, aerial hopes that there will be bread for all. And because it is yours, you send rain the way it pleases you, drop by drop, in innocent plumes, barely on sandals, in a sweet pit-a-pat; or else, you fill the buckets and open the faucets of those rivers up there, hastening deluges that you sign (in Aramaic?) with the instant calligraphy of lightning.

It rains. I feel sorry for those with cloudy eyes because they cannot see the deposits of water through which God appears for an instant or for forty days.

※❦❧❧❦❧❦❧❦❦※

Give Us Today Our Daily Bread

Here I have millions of petitions that have arrived today. I am glad when they ask me for bread; it is a sign that those who used to be children would like to be like children again. You stop being a child when you do not ask for anything anymore.

"Give us today our bread. A piece of bread is so simple. We are not asking you for dishes à la carte, the menu of exclusive restaurants, but just bread, popular and homemade, white within, golden crusted, corn bread, wheat bread, or rye bread."

"That bread which you think so simple is so complex. Because bread, just one piece of bread, is the result of mixing laws of nature, obligations of justice, the labor of human hands, and the love of this, your Father. In order for bread to reach the mouth, there was a real need for spring, fall, sun, water, ears of grain, stems, sickles, barns, mills, ovens, and a sleepy baker who, at five o'clock in the morning, his white cap on and violet rings under his eyes, would knead and cook."

"Give us today our daily bread."

"Yes, I will give you precisely today's bread, not tomorrow's, much less bread to stockpile. No, it is good that you have to ask for it each day because, otherwise, the bread would harden."

"Give us today our bread."

Be Perfect

"Listen, Father, I am considering whether the following recommendation — or is it a command? — of Christ should go with a question mark or an exclamation point: 'Be perfect as your Father who is in heaven is perfect' (Matthew 5:48). How difficult. Because *perfect* means holy, the giant of virtue. And neither you nor he is satisfied with less. You do not tolerate the lukewarm, the mediocre, the athlete who is not up to the mark.

"And then that 'be perfect' that encompasses all of us, simply all. Perfection is not a diamond ring that only the elite can buy on Fifth Avenue. Perfect must be the monk who rises at dawn to sing psalms in Gregorian chant and the worker who takes care of the furnaces during the night. Each one becomes a saint in his or her place, as birds become birds in their nests.

"And how perfect must one become, really? Like Francis of Assisi, sealed, tattooed, stamped with the five stigmata? No, another is the model. Like Theresa of Jesus, that white and brown deer by the seraphim wounded?

No, higher, much higher. As the heavenly Father is perfect."

"Lord, don't you think it is just too much for this fragile littleness that we are? How will a child climb this immense rugged mountain?"

"Our Father will lead the child by the hand. Let yourself be led."

A Concert of Sparrows

You know that the sparrow is the best known of all the birds since it has followed civilized people throughout the entire world. Ornithologists call it in Latin *passer domesticus*, the house sparrow, like a domesticated bird. Ladies loved to have orchestral sparrows at home, until the gabble of television sets frightened them.

They are small, measuring about six inches from one extreme to another; their beak is conical, short and somehow convex; the wings, wide and short; the tail, medium sized and square; and the plumage, brown like the habits of monks. Their menu is well balanced according to dietetic experts: they eat grain, insects, herbs, and fruits. May it profit them well, my little children.

At that time when my Son lived in Galilee, a sparrow was worth half an as. The as was a small Roman copper coin, equivalent to less than a penny, a farthing, that is, nothing. Who buys sparrows? Cheap and singing sparrows for a farthing.

"Why do you tell us about sparrows, Eternal Father?"

"To show you how much I love you, just as Jesus told you: 'Are not two sparrows sold for a farthing? However, not even one of them (so small and insignificant) falls on the ground without my Father's allowing it. And you, the very hairs of your head are all numbered. Be not afraid, therefore, you are worth more than all the sparrows in the world'" (Matthew 10:29-30).

The Parable of the Son
Who Went Far Away

There was a father who lived in Guadalajara, Mexico, with his two sons. Alas, a small family does not always know how to live best. The firstborn son was a good boy, never gave his father a headache. But the younger one was a handful, *un calavera*, as they say down there, that is, frivolous and irresponsible, as is sometimes the case with juniors. So much so that one day, just like that, without more ado, he went to his father and told him, "Dad, give me the part of the inheritance that is mine."

"But, my son, I'm not yet dying."

The poor old man could not help it and signed a big check for him, one of those with many zeros on the right side.

The younger son left for the States. New York, San Francisco, Las Vegas. In a few weeks he threw away his inheritance. A nightclub with blonde and red-haired women, the Sheraton with indoor swimming pool and breakfast in bed, gambling machines that swallowed more dollars than they vomited, and he lost it all.

Well, in such situations one has to be willing to work doing anything, like any other illegal alien, to work on a farm, taking care of Mr. Smith's pigs, all so pink and so well-fed with vitamins, those pigs of a man who exploited the son with starvation wages. He was starving indeed; for the first time in his life he found out what hunger was (which, by the way, is a very useful experience for those who have everything and live in luxury). The day passed with an insipid hot dog and a warm Coca-Cola.

That night he began to think. What on earth am I doing here, starving to death, when even my father's driver in Mexico is having a much better time than I? Tomorrow I'm going back home, if I have to hitchhike all the way.

Gaunt, his jeans all washed out, penniless, a piggish odor all over him, he arrived as best he could at his father's home on the avenue.

His father, who was at the door — waiting, hopeful — saw him coming, and a shudder of joy overtook him. He came immediately out and there was no need to tell his son that he forgave him. The son was quickly smothered with a big hug and dozens of kisses.

"Dad, forgive me, I don't have the face to call myself your son."

"Hey, you, Nicolás, don Mateo, tell everyone; and

bring from my son's closet the best suit and put it on him; bring also a ring, tell the kitchen to prepare a banquet, I mean, a real banquet. Ah, and don't forget to hire the best mariachi."

"Dad, why have you never given a party for my friends?" demanded the faithful son. "I have never conducted myself badly. Why do you do this for him and not for me?"

"You have always been with me. But this other son of mine was lost, he was a profligate, and today I have found him."

There, by the shores of Lake Chapala near Guadalajara, while the waves knocked each other down, breaking their crests, Jesus assured the villagers listening to him, "Such is the joy my Father feels when a sinner repents. There is no father so much a father as he."

Father, Why Hast Thou Forsaken Me?

The fatal word in six voices

1

Oh, fatal word! Why have you been uttered? Why were you not kept inside the chest? Did not Christ know that you would be used against him? How could his contemporaries see in him, in this man, sunk in pain, the Messiah who would save his people from worldly humiliations? And how could one not find in that cry an argument that could be used by those who in the future would deny his divinity? If he is God, how can he say that his God is abandoning him? Yes, fatal word that will be till the end of the world a scandal for the faith of the world.

But adorable word also for those who believe. It unveils the mystery of the incarnation and the radical self-emptying of the Word made flesh. And that Word is indeed a scandal. But the whole Gospel is a scandal. He saves the world contradicting it. And at the end he will overturn all things.

Charles Journet, *Les Sept Paroles du Christ* (Paris: Seuil, 1952). Excerpt translated by Alvaro de Silva.

2

And then there was heard in the thick air, in the silence of darkness, these words, "Eli, Eli, Lama Sabachthani?" That is to say, "My God, my God, why hast thou forsaken me?"

This was the first verse of a psalm that Christ had repeated to himself many times because he had found there so many presages of his life and of his death. . . . The supplications of this prophetic psalm, which recall so closely the Man of Sorrows of Isaiah, rose from the wounded heart of the crucified man as the last expression of his dying humanity.

Giovanni Papini, *Life of Christ*, trans. Dorothy Canfield Fisher (New York: Harcourt, Brace and Co., 1923; many printings), pp. 372-73.

3

Jesus was not hanging on the cross to utter metaphors. If he says that the Father is abandoning him, it is because, really, somehow he is being abandoned. Perhaps we shall never understand the how, but he experienced it indeed as a true distance. However, what was the dimension and meaning of this distance? The key to the mystery is that, in that moment, Christ is about to accomplish the work of redemption and is assuming all the sins of the world. He is not sinning but making sin really his own. Truly it is now that he who has no sin becomes radically one of us. If that barrier of evil is what distinguishes him from us, now, out of love, he will jump over it. And he will pay for it in solitude, in that terrible solitude in which he really experiences his Father's distance from the very center of his soul. But his cry is not from despair. It is a wrenching lament, but a loving one.

Jose Luis Martín Descalzo,
Vida y misterio de Jesús de Nazaret,
(Salamanca: Sígueme, 1988).
Excerpt translated by Alvaro de Silva.

4

In a loud voice, which was astonishing, since crucifixion paralyses the lungs and clamps the throat, he cried, "Eloi, eloi, lamma sabachtani" (Matthew 27:46). The words were in his mother tongue, Aramaic; they are the opening of the Messianic Psalm 22. . . . The Psalm is not only an imploring cry which the suffering flesh sends out in protest, and it is not expressing doubt but supreme confidence, for "thou didst make me hope when I was upon my mother's breasts. . . . Be not far from me, for trouble is near."

Henry Daniel-Rops, *Jesus and his Times*
(New York: Dutton, 1954), p. 552.

5

The Father abandoned Jesus not by distancing himself from him but by depriving him of his help. Jesus makes his own the first words of Psalm 22, which, all in all, rather expresses a splendid trust. Only Omnipotence can reach down to this impotence; its extreme possibility touches the exact limit of what is impossible, that which no creature will ever reach. No one will ever know, as the Son knows, what it is to be abandoned by the Father, because no one but the Son has known what it is to be one with the Father.

José María Cabodevilla, *Cristo vivo*
(Madrid: Editorial Católica, 1963).
Excerpt translated by Alvaro de Silva.

6

Christ's cry was of abandonment, which He felt standing in a sinner's place, but it was not of despair. . . . Man turned away from God; now He, who was God united personally with a human nature, willed to feel in that human nature that awful wrench as if He himself were guilty. . . . It was, therefore, the moment when leaning on nails he stood at the brink of hell in the name of all sinners. As He entered upon the extreme penalty of sin, which is separation from God, it was fitting that His eyes be filled with darkness and His soul with loneliness.

Fulton J. Sheen, *Life of Christ*
(New York: McGraw-Hill, 1958), p. 452.

My Son's Return

It was midday on earth, and in heaven eternity, when my
Son took off from the Mount of Olives and gained altitude.
It was as if a beam of light kept on growing and growing,
making the blue sky forever blue. His disciples half closed
their eyes to see him better, to keep on seeing him. No one
had yet invented field glasses and telescopes. What a pity.

Breaking through the pure air, he joyfully ascended.
Up and up he went. It was like the small white trail left by a
space rocket. Then, a cloud crossed the cosmic silence and
enveloped it in its vapors.

Alas, coveted cloud,
how rich you are up there,
how poor and blind
alas, you leave us down here.

You can imagine the jubilant celebration when my Son
arrived home. Welcome, sit down at my right side.

He was dressed in a suit made of flesh, the only glorious flesh that had ever entered eternity. He could not bring from the earth a better trophy than those hands of a crafts-man with the marks of nails. Cherubim were absolutely as-tonished seeing veins, eyes, lips,

and beard and hair like the sun's mane
and fair and bare his feet like silver.

<hr>

The Hesitant Light

One evening — the light didn't know whether to leave or stay, afraid of undoing its transparency — one evening, I, the Eternal Father, went down incognito to chat with a child playing with a top.

"What would you like to be when you grow up?"

"God," the child answered decidedly.

"You would not please anyone. If there is sun, people begin to say, 'My God, let it rain.' And God puts the sun back in its box and it begins to rain. And then people say,

'My God, let the sun come out and make the downpour stop.' And poor God, who loves everybody, doesn't seem to satisfy anyone."

"Would you like to be God?" the child asked.

I looked at the top and made it spin.

The Appointment of Francis of Assisi

Peace and good, Francis, my son.

Having been informed that some groups of people on earth lack a patron saint who might be their model and intercessor, we have determined to appoint you, effective immediately and well assured of your joyful obedience, patron of the following:

1. Considering that one day, on your way up the mountain, you bent down to cut a yellow daisy and immediately abandoned the idea, saying to the flower, "God has sent you to embellish the fields; let us not take creatures away from their mission," you shall be from now on patron of

ecologists and like-minded people who defend the inno-
cence of the air, of the water, and of the forests so that your
brothers and sisters may live in a world that is visible, audi-
ble, breathable, likeable, and all in all delightful;

2. Considering that you were friend of a falcon who ate
from your dish and who with gray eyes looked sweetly
upon you and, realizing that you were sick, would not
wake you up at midnight but would wait till dawn that you
might pray Lauds, we constitute you patron of ornitholo-
gists, of veterinarians, of beast lovers, of humane societies,
of workers in zoological parks, and likewise patron of cem-
eteries and crematories for animals, provided they are
modest and not luxurious;

3. Considering that you went through towns and cities
singing peace and love with a clean voice and a well-played
cittern — long before the "peace & love" theme of the
flower children — we declare you patron of active nonvio-
lence, which is the only war that conquers injustice without
spilling blood.

Given in eternity, and therefore not dated.

With the immutable love of

ETERNAL FATHER

An Unpublished Letter
to Mother Teresa
of Calcutta

I was thinking of writing a letter to you, my dear daughter Teresa; but for several reasons I finally decided not to send it to earth.

In the first place, since you are traveling the world around serving your poor, there was the danger that the letter would not reach you anywhere.

In the second place, since you barely read with those tiny eyes of yours now so tired, I prefer that you make good use of the little light remaining in them to continue looking into the dispossessed and sick, those open books so very few people read.

In the third place, were you to receive a letter from heaven, there would certainly appear one of those devil's advocates who, when the time came, would make trouble for you in the cause of your canonization.

So, be left simply like that, with your sari, your sandals,

your wrinkles, the sick you help, the light breath of life that you are.

Your Eternal Father who, rather than writing to you, wishes much more to see you.

❦❦❦❦❦❦❦

Prayer for a Son

My son is a big chunk of flesh. He doesn't think. He hasn't learned my name. A son who cannot say "father," who will never say it. "Mentally retarded," that's what the doctors call him euphemistically. I know that he is a watch no one can wind up, a watch without hands.

A cage without a bird. A bird without a song. An electric lamp that doesn't give light. Who unplugged the wire where the energy comes from? Like a dog howling in the night, he is sunk in a tunnel of instincts. Sometimes he shouts, groans, as rudimentary as a wild beast. Eats, sleeps. The poor life of the senses. And his fugitive eyes, like old windows in a ruined house.

Lord, you do the thinking for those beings that have no thought. You guide irrational creatures toward their last ends to them unknown. You think for the star and for the dove with feet like a star. You direct their steps toward the harmony of the universe.

Help me imitate you in my own way. Help me be a father to this creature without light, this son of yours and of mine for whom I must think and discern. Guiding this life that knows not its destiny, let me share in your wisdom and be for him your Providence on earth.

Please teach me to guide those who walk in greater darkness than mine.

❁❁❁❁❁❁❁

I, a Child, Accuse Myself

Eternal Father smiled, hiding his smile in his beard. He was browsing the diary of a priest in which, without writing down names so as not to violate the sacramental seal, the priest had written the confessions of some children. Sins? You will decide, Eternal Father.

"I accuse myself of being very disobeyed." (Blessed are those who change active for passive voice.)

"I accuse myself, father, that I beat up my friends." (If he does that to his friends, what will he not do to his enemies?)

"I also accuse myself of faking I was sick to miss school."

"I accuse myself, father, of disobeying my parents and my mothers." (Boy, how many mothers do you have?)

"I am sorry of having tell swears and curses." (This one's grammar may be as serious a problem as his cursing.)

"I accuse myself, father, that I gave my dog hot peppers to make him angry."

"I accuse myself that when my mom tells me to take a bath, I don't take one." (Blessed the clean of heart, and of feet and hands too.)

"I accuse myself that I love my cat more than I love my grandma." (Let's hope the cat doesn't tell the grandmother.)

"I accuse myself, father, that I was mad at Santa Claus; I asked him for a video camera and he left me a bag of candy."

If Eternal Father had tears, perhaps he would have

wept out of pure tenderness upon listening to this confession of a seven-year-old girl:

"I accuse myself of stealing a flower to bring it to the Virgin. . . ."

Fantasy

Eternal Father was taking a walk in heaven when, passing close by Gabriel, luminous as a river standing up, he said to praise him, "You are an angel."

"And you are Heaven," answered Gabriel.

The Father then approached a group of souls interchanging ideas about words. (They had been grammarians and language teachers on earth.)

"Excuse me for interrupting your scholarly conversation, but the day will come when children will have to learn the meaning of words they no longer understand. Children in India will ask, What is hunger? Those of South Africa, What does *racial segregation* mean? Those of Hiroshima will

wonder, What is this thing called "atomic bomb"? South
American children will ask, What is this "foreign debt"?
And all the children in all the schools will ask, What is war?

"Their teachers will have to answer them, 'These are
archaic expressions, names of things fallen out of use, like
stagecoaches, top hats, armors of errant knights. These
words don't mean anything anymore. Now we live in the
world that the Eternal Father wants to have. Please, ex-
punge those words from the dictionary.'"

My Answer to Your "Our Father"

Dear Diary,
    When they open you and read, I want my children to
know that each time they pray to me in the "Our Father," I
answer them with the "My Child":

> My child who art on earth,
>   troubled, tempted, alone.

I know your name, understand
　　that I love you.
You are not alone but I dwell in you,
　　heir to my kingdom.
That you may do my will,
　　count always with me.
You will have bread this day, don't worry,
　　but do share it with others.
I forgive your trespasses against me,
　　so many,
　　provided you forgive
　　those who trespass against you.
That you may not fall into temptation,
　　take hold strongly of my hand,
　　and I will deliver you from evil,
　　poor and beloved child of mine.

To My Atheistic Children

I want to tell you, before anything else, that I love you with all my heart, that I respect your freedom, and that, even if you do not think at all about me, I do think a lot about you. (More so now, perhaps, when your denial of me, so insistently made, is a way of remembering me.) Please, do not make of your atheism a dogma of faith.

Can a finger cover up the sun? What is difficult is not to discover me but to cover me up, hiding me from view. Look at the universe, look at life, look at the human body, and the symphony of the stars: there you see huge neon signs announcing me. Who has ever invented a decisive argument against my existence?

No, there aren't any pure atheists. You, like all other human beings, need to love, have an insatiable hunger for light and for providing meaning to the few years that life lasts. Denying the Absolute, you are left with small things, like sparkling fireflies that soon die out and then only the night remains. You dismantle the foundations, the walls and the roof, and live unsheltered lives. It hurts me to see you thus unprotected, your disturbing feeling of evanescence, perhaps even of pride and egocentrism.

In the face of this vacuum, this silence of God or his death, you look for substitutes; and thus you deify nature, humanity, the state, technology, money; you make idols of the athlete and the pretty blonde girl at the microphone — pocket gods that never fully satisfy the infinite restlessness in your soul.

Take a look at the sunflower, a heliotropic plant, a plant that throughout the day rotates its corolla following the sun's path. Man is "theotropic," looking for God even without knowing and even when denying that he is looking for me. But I do not accuse you. I wait. I am patient. I love.

Father, into Your Hands
I Commend My Spirit

Father,

Let me write down a few lines in your diary before the day comes to an end. Because there is already little sun left. The clock does not give the time anymore, it just takes it away.

I know that you are going to come to judge me in the very instant of my departure. Wake me up if you find me asleep, under anesthesia, unconscious, practically brainless, with that useless blink that is called artificial life.

I am a human being, do you see me? I am indeed a real human being. Kneaded in sinful clay. Look at me, Father, just in case I cannot see you then. When the serum, the pacemaker, the radiations, and the sedatives will be of no use at all, I shall have no other strength but the strength you'll give me.

Come, talk to me, come back to talk to me. What time is it? It is the hour of the fever, of the lost heartbeat, of fear, of the heart gone mad. What time is it? It is night. Come by, say one word, the one you and I like most. The hour of my passing from this world has come. Where to? My sin is always before me. Are you there, Father? Look at him. It is the agony. It is the death rattle, muddy gaze, open mouth, cold, each time colder. The doctor says, "he is dead." And you, what do you say, Father? Say the word I hope for: *My child, poor and beloved child of mine.*

Come, Blessed of My Father

No one knows the date of the final day but I. It is my secret that I never reveal. But I want to write something in these pages about it. I can assure you that it will be a beautiful day.

Don't you like to see those passengers arriving at railroad stations and airports? On one side, the waves of those arriving with their suitcases and great expectations; on the other, the faces of relatives and friends who keep on turning and turning to find the long-awaited persons. Before going through customs, each one is alone and anxious; then comes the encounter, the embraces, the kisses.

Think, my dear diary, that on the final day, millions and millions of travelers will arrive at the immense railroad station of the City of God, at the airport terminals of the Eternal Father. Imagine the voices, the shouts of joy, the smiles, the embraces. Relatives and friends, ancestors from faraway centuries, and so many people with whom my sons and daughters were united even though they had never met.

"At last I met my father," the posthumous son will say. "I always wanted so much to meet Teresa of Avila, Bach, Miguel de Cervantes, Leonardo da Vinci." "There is Adam, let me say hello to him." "Look at that rose of snow, golden rose, ivory rose, Hail Mary." What madness of joy!

I assure you that the encounter is going to be pure madness: all the world waiting for all the world in the last railroad station for trains arriving home. Come, enter, meet each other, love one another, stay with me forever. And right then and there the great feast will begin and never end.